Home: *विरह दरभंगा से दिल्ली तक*

Asim Mudgal © 2024

All rights reserved. No parts of this publication may be reproduced, stored in a retrieval system, or transmitted, in any form or otherwise, without the author's prior permission.

Asim Mudgal © 2024

This book is sold subject to the condition that it shall not, by way of trade or otherwise, be lent, re-sold, hired out, or otherwise circulated without the author's prior consent in any form of binding or cover other than that in which it is published.

Where I Begin?

Remembrance is pious.
Death is also pious.
What to remember?
What to die for?

प्रेमो-अस्तीत्वो भवः।

Contents

Some questions to ask:

What is your मनोकामना?

Why is it your मनोकामना?

How is it your मनोकामना?

Answer this and keep a notepad.

Chapter 1: *दरभंगा*

Jix, [01-08-2023 14:54]
Every dose of kisses
Is a sweet fragrance
That tangles around my neck
How sweet, how funny.

Jix, [01-08-2023 19:05]
Hey, I am a poet,
I don't know grammar,
I want to learn grammar,
But my mathematics is tragic,
So I stopped learning grammar.

So, I am not a poet,
I am a looser,
Queer Poets are looser as fuck,
People in India consider queer poetry equivalent to
heterosexual poems.

Jix, [01-08-2023 19:11]
There's a boy,
The boy is going to pee,

Suddenly snakes arrive and bite his pee-e.

Jix, [01-08-2023 19:31]
1. There are two people,
They cringe,
Seeing two men kiss.

Jix, [02-08-2023 10:19]
2. There's a deathbed in the corner,
And I sleep on the couch,
Comfortable and Quiet,
Death bed noises,
Telling me to make him my home.

Jix, [02-08-2023 10:23]
3. There's a muffin in the corner,
And I eat Karela,
Muffins make noises,
Telling me to be his sweet.

Jix, [02-08-2023 19:35]
Sleeveless men walking through corridors,
Making my heart pounds a Hundred shores.
Corridors, Corridors, make my heart assured,
Two bites, ten roles.
One of an abuser,
One of the touch players,
One of a foot massager,
One of the body players,
One of the finger sawyers,
One of the nipples lickers,
One of the shoulders healer,
One of the chest dwellers,

One of the kissers,
One of the abusers turned lover.

Monologue After Buring my two non-poetic books, "You Are Not My Type Honey," and "World Is Full of Paper, And I am Writing a Letter To Him." (Previously named, "Peeping Away," changed it after reading Agha Shahid Ali.

Jix, [04-08-2023 17:37]
1. I saw a white falcon today,
I dreamt of living in the suburbs,
There is no ancient Bard, who can take me my home,
I am a California dream, living Italian renaissance,
Spanish foe, who cares, I am still a missing history.

Jix, [04-08-2023 17:44]
2. I live in a small town, called Darbhanga,
Waiting for my dawn,
I watch a moon, sky, and a Harahi lake in the courtyard of my district, I am Maithil a Mithilanchal nivasi,
Who doesn't know Maithil literature, Who Is stolen bird, likely to drown,
I am a LGBT Bard, with no money for Oxford to be called a scholar,
My Poetic language is out of the linguistics era and my grammar trembling,
I want to swim in the Spanish Ocean, and walk on Italian streets,
The preface says, I will be writing there,
But who reads my darbhanga courtyard of old red flowers, and a Newborn neem tree?

Jix, [04-08-2023 17:49]
3. The red flowers in my garden are offered to the goddess Kali,
She is the queen of Mithalanchal culture, She stays in a temple built on the great darbhanga maharaja's grave,
She is honourable, and I am dry fruit for offerings,
I am not even Mohini,
I am not even Kalidasa, who wrote poems, by staying all night reading Maithil literature.
I want to be a king of my queer culture, I wish I were a Kalidasa or Kali, but the world calls me Kali,
Yes, soon, I will decide the end of my own world,
I am red flowers of my garden.

Jix, [04-08-2023 17:57]
4. Sitting in my room, which is not mine, I imagine a French kiss and a Spanish boyfriend, maybe I am a post-colonial Bard, caged in my country.

I am still a poor migratory bird travelling States to complete my education, I am looking for Masters in literature, and I got history in my dictionary, I wasn't a poet, 2018 was a mistaken writing journey I started, and now it's 2023, even Taylor swifts songs can't make me lyrical, that's why I am practising Indian English listening to Prateek Kuhad.

Jix, [04-08-2023 18:02]
5. I want to stop now.
I am still writing in the same language
No vocabulary no Patience
No depth No career

Let's forget there existed a phase of writing in my
life,
Or maybe remember the time when writing gave me
my first crush, my first boyfriend, and my inner
peace.

It helped me put myself vulnerable,
I wrote three diaries recalling my past, helping me get
through life at 19, I am 23 now,
I am still beautiful,
Beautifully dead.

6. In search of finding the language of the age,
I am rushing like an 18th-century rage.
I won't be remembered that closely because I have
surpassed my 18th birthday,
I pictured Mr Chatterton
And questions my entire age
Am I living in 21st-century Darbhanga or England's
Romantic age?

7. Dear Sylvia Plath,
You and mine Daddy are on the same page,
The only difference Is that I call him "Papa",
Like you, I too feared him in my childhood domestic
course,
The only difference is that I confronted him in the
coronavirus lockdown antidote,
Yes, you would know that coronavirus arrived in the
world after your death, and brought confrontation to
lots of houses and divorce too.
Babes, my head calls you the immortal queen with
immortal poems,

I couldn't make it 30 yet,
So no time for dying, Making me upset.

Chapter 2: *दिल्ली*

लोककथा

There's a death bed in the corner,
And I sleep on the couch,
Comfortable and Quiet,
Death bed noises,
Telling me to make him my home.

When I was born
I didn't know walking street would be self-conscious act
What's man's walk?
What's woman's walk?
When everything is a human craft.
One day I died like a flower in my garden
Some people said I am murderer
That I killed myself.
Two days later a milkman arrives at my door
He smells my blood
He second guess his stinct and says
The body was decaying for years.
Three days later an old woman arrives at my door
My mother brought her a tea
They sit together in a courtyard and take small sips
The woman says I saw him dancing naked, I shut my window and called my husband
He called me the boy is troubled soul.
On 9th day, the police man said, the boy was gay, he probably killed by his date.

It's week two of my AUD campus life,
So far It's quiet at the moment,
I Don't know why I am sitting in the shade of big
branch tree,
First of impression of which was It's canteen area
But this area isn't canteen
It's the sitting spot and surroundings of breeze
The wind that's blowing through is what makes this
place special, I guess.

The art of traveling in slow walking metro...
Why he left we don't know
Why he turned back we don't know
Why he stopped we don't know
Why he is standing at the gate even though there's
seats around, we don't know
We don't know his past, present and future.

We know once he lived
Once he talked
Once he danced to a song
Once he had a chocolate ice-cream
Once he joined the MBA course
But we don't know why he is travelling in the slow-
walking metro at 9:53 on October 4th 2023.

Body

My body is a trip
Tripping into the crowd of my village
Breathing through stars on the terrace
I ask my fourteen-year self
How ashamed I am of my being
ashamed of sexuality
ashamed of identity
ashamed of my manhood
ashamed of my gender
ashamed of my next fifteen, sixteen, seventeen,
eighteen, twenty, twenty-one, twenty-two, twenty-
three,
What is love?
Just another body
And I haven't learnt the art of it.
I am closing my doors to the village
No death can call me to their grave
Neither do mine.

What is social anxiety?
Art of not being social
Mixing in the crowd
Losing courage at the right moment.
Do you have tears seeing a dead body?
Do you feel tears seeing your lover?
Perhaps you have lost all of your senses
the touch, sight, hear, taste, and breath
wait for the right moment when you will drown in
your closeted bedroom

For your favourite me time
Don't worry people will always question your social
anxiety with your love.
It's not fire that travels through the ocean
All these are philosophical sagas of tele shop and
films from old times
is not fitting the village scene.
If you can't serve a plate on the ground.
You are women far from the ground.
Here only the dead cry, speak, feel, and taste.
Living is an apology.

Violence in my life

I experienced two forms of violence in my life
One, of my cousin-brother.
One, of my mother.
This violence that took place in the school bus
The other that took in my home
In both, I am a statue
Perpetually gazing
I wish he would have listened to what elders said on
deeds of being in school,
Discipline, politeness, and quietness. I thought in my
mind on my homely bed.
I wish she could not have listened to what elders said
about the deeds of a married woman,
adjustment, sacrifice, and care. I think now in my
mind lying on a homely bed in my pg.
My colleague at school said that if they had a brother
engaged in a fight, they would have fought like men
for their brother.
They were right. And I suffered from a manhood
crisis.
What is the story of a storyteller?
What is the poetry of the poet?
That violence and sadness perpetuate in their gaze
of The most anisochronic phase.

Summer In M1

My room temperature is higher than any AC bill.
Still, I am living in a mini cooler I bought at 999 and a fan on
I tried and felt a serious headaches
So considerate and calm
I went for a walk in the Gtb market.
I felt a headache
Again so considerate and calm
I returned home
In my pg, I feel navigating
From hot Summer to wanting monsoon the weather I don't like,
But today I am swelling my gland in dryness for muddy water after rain
So I can walk Again
Surviving to live
Saving extra bills from someone else's pocket money.
This is a story of every male guy who desires a male body.
Adjustment, discipline, and prospects (of course of future).

Poetry From Local Darbhanga

I Don't write poetry for longing
Neither for peacefulness
Neither to create a memory that will bind into one
I write poems for staying back in frames
In pictures
In moments that there was someone who stayed back
In memory of my existence, in place, time, and
reassurance.

Mediaoting

Every guy I met
has been caught in the camera's eye
I am assuming they might have been looking for me
now
Lost on periphery
Now I am the centre of all attraction
Curiously hiding all the momentary touching
sensation I experienced some of the night
All my mornings are endless stalking
Afternoon studying through gazes of my cultural
identity and skinny body
Evening, I am pulsating on my curios tool making
Porno graphia in my head
At night I stay calm like any wind of summer.

Rules

To a Partially blind guy, I matched on the hinge
What if we have met in person
One who can't see through my eyes when closer
It is a more romantic film
I ever discovered
Rest all where fantasy I was Peeping Away.

If Maithili was my love language

1. हमर नाम विचलित अछि।

   हम भटक गेल छी।

   कोनाक हम अपन कथा सुनाऊ

   जब हमर जीवन भेल पहाड

   उनको नइँ हमर चिन्ता

   जे कहयत छेथिन अपने क विहार।

2. एहन फूटल सौभाग्य ककरो नइँ होय

   हम तँ बेमतलबक चिन्तन म छी

   अस्ल म तँ चिन्तन ओकरा करयके चाहि जे हमरा सऽ रूसल

   अछि।

Navigating Semester-system in Masters

It's not a new story,
It's everyone's story.
But this story is from *Queer* Guy.

1. Killing a Curious cat is an art.
   And one at the top of the grading system knows it best.
   I lost all my enthusiasm, reading habits and curiosity at the beginning of the Second semester.
   And is still continuing so far.
2. The first moment I entered GTB Nagar
   Was never for a job
   It was for an opportunity
   Opportunity to complete my Masters degree
   Opportunity to complete degree to become financially independent
   Because for the Man I am
   Deep inside me
   Demands an answers
   From the blots of societal norms
   To be a father
   A brother
   A son
   And an employed adult.
   I needed everything once I started staying in GTB

As a PG student in single-room
Counting the days and covering the night
To see how beautiful I aged at that time in the
years ahead.
3. Despite all the marrows,
Tinkling occasional sorrows,
I am living,
The way you are,
With some Lemon, Salt, and Sugar,
It's bitter-sweet dreams,
And I am living.
4. Sometimes I feel there's a Western eye gazing
through my Indian answer sheet,
I feel drowning whenever I see grades below
average,
They have to understand that if they are
educated abroad, it does not give them a pass
in understanding Indian literary education,
I am drowning in mentality,
Look what those eyes are doing me,
Some people left the course,
I see personal prejudices too excised during
grading
I fear what this department is made of
The so-called 'Oxfordian' model is playing
war with the 'Indian' model
Then those eyes will picture one candidate
and attribute them all the genius quality
Those 'exceptional' and 'miraculous' genius---
they will call them
Rest will dwell on so-called Lockean
Consciousness
Practice Death Before Death
Or Death happens.
5. My boy got his favourite toys

And he plays with like a Hollywood Singer
I watch him stay at home
Behind a closed door
Singing a lullaby
Out of course
I laugh hard at my grief
He is too sweet and bitter
I am downgraded grades playing with his
smooth gift.

6. This is the gayest lamenting...
    Only merry and broken heart
    Is here to relish
    Every beat and piece.

7. I often imagine myself playing in the
    churchyard of my hometown
    Asking Jesus to bring back my childhood
    crush, If any.
    I often imagine myself visiting the museum in
    my hometown
    That same museum where the sun sets in the
    evening lake.
    I often imagine walking quiet streets leading
    to the LNMU campus,
    Seeing all those Yellowish, Red, and White
    monarchy buildings saying goodbye to long-
    lost history.
    I often imagine myself bringing life to that
    history
    I see myself lamenting a picture of myself
    sitting close to Harahi Lake
    And when the sun sets, I walk Quietly smiling
    to the narrowed lanes to my home.

8. I feel I am running from my classroom
    corridors,

The only reason I sit on the first bench in
every classroom
Because it makes me feel close to the window
and door at the same time
It gives me perspective:
Why are people cycling on the road
Why isn't there anything Philosophical in my
eyes through my classroom window— I am
not Wordsworth, John Keats, Blake or
Coleridge,
I am a random guy from Darbhanga
Early break, and I am home
How would I like to run away from my school
door
Not that all kids are judging me
I just want to come back home
Maybe it's just a mere battle I am fighting for
Score well and keep moving ahead.

9. My boyfriend died in the car crash,
And I imagine him at every metro station
Is he looking at me, Or Am I looking for him,
Two eyes that dwell apart
Are synchronising.

English is my love language

Dear lover,
I am writing A note in the English language from England
Where my diction fluctuates between my regional tongue
Is the language I learnt
Getting slapped and pencil intertwined around my fingers
Grades above average
Down below my belly
A cold warm fluttering
Makes my pronunciation calmer
Articles perfect
Mirroring the dark room
Whose sentence structure is always white, pink and brown
Sometimes there's blue to match the color of the sky
A cassette from my closet
Going in my closets.
After brief: I am not here to perfect
I will learn
I will be myself
In the flow
In the confidence
In the meeting
In the university
In my previous college
In my school
At my home

See how much violence I have crossed down the lane
of my childhood
To write a note in the English language from
England
Every time I think, read and write in this language
reminds me
How much colonisers have given us
Is the same violence I am doing every night to mark
my debut in your twitched heart
Only to hear me once
How expensive I am now
Then I was yesterday.

Mathura and Vrindavan

The pink frame of Prem Mandir
Reminds me of my blue sky
In heavy rain and eating lunch at Apni Rasoyi.
After Tripping around Mathura, Gokul, and
Goverdhan,
Mathura, a temple dwelling apart from Aurangzeb
Majid, seems to have a complicated history.
Gokul, Nand Gaon of money policy where every
aesthetic Darshan is rated at a maximum of 2600.
Goverdhan, an interesting place where Rajasthan
makes an appearance for one kilometre in 12
kilometre Parikrama.
We reached to Banke Bihari
And Waited 45 minutes barefoot on a road playing
with rainy mud
At five it was a long queue
At five-forty five it was all inside
Entering there at the moment
From the entrance, our eyes were alert searching for
black Idol.
Banke Bihari was a crowded mess
The storm of people throwing you out from gate
number four
I wasn't able to throw flowers in my mind
Neither was I able to offer Parsad bought at the shop
in 400.
It was nothing like the classroom discussion of
beauty
How we can't meet eye to eye in him

How some ruler (I don't remember) went captivated
seeing eyes of him
Why purdah is done to hide his mystical beauty luring
the eyes of visitors
It wasn't even eye to eye meeting
Rather A far away distant bliss.
Eye fades
In a blue sky
And pink frame of memory
Saying Krishna is not in Vrindavan
And yet I am gopi attaining shringar rasa with him.
The Lyrical Pasts of Pre-Modern Poetry from South
Asia
Makes beauty of eye overexaggeration
Room of Sublime
I surrender.

Navigating Through Cricket Culture of India

30.06.2024
Watching cricket in my teenagehood
Reminded me of its features
That is manly
Among men, you are trained to build your reciprocity
I learnt neither of the dos of a cricketer and cricket fan.
I heard they used synonyms of "Chake" as a "chaka" when the camera pans on the Idol of social media.
I already had a brief moment with cricket in my teenage years
Fielding off and on
Bating or battling the bats on the ground
Hurting the eyes in class three pinick while catching the ball
Visiting my Bua to throw balls like Malinga among the room Renter who used to play cricket.
I did that sort of Indian phenomenon where I prayed and took an oath to offer ladoo to Malech Mardini Mandir at Mirzapur if India won the World Cup again. I did offer that the next day.
It's far ahead of my time with cricket.
Now I look back at it and the homophobia culture that it endures.
It Makes my pleasure and liking a merely motivated consumption of manhood in my strangely acting veins.

It's only when veins clothe you realize you have been born again.
In here it's one: many
And when a dystopia hits, the minority always sinks.
The economic cricketry culture always wins.

2.7.2024

Visiting NKS Hospital at Gulabi Bagh Second Time
for my father's eye check-up
Reminds me how important it is to have an eye.
One that teaches the vigilantes not to shit anywhere
One that teaches a researcher to preserve what's true
One that teaches the leader not to engage in Verbal
masquerade
One that teaches the models to look up when camera
shutters in frames
One teaches the explorer that beauty is not in the
beholder's eyes but the trial to extract it in the mind.
An eye for an eye
Sounds revolutionary
In every drop of serum
That proliferates in its veins
It Sucks up the dirty
To say "No" to every time people call you mad.

While Talking To Kashmiri Guy On Instagram.

The Summer Was Real This Summer.
Even In Delhi, It Was Warm and Suffocating
Warmness Outside and Inside.
So lured and offbeat.
Like a doormat surviving on foot tips
The economy of my body is sweating in the dust.
So I ran away from my only PG home on the 18th of
July
At my Bua's house to feel the breeze of the AC.

What is a Memory?

What is a memory
A memory of love
The loving
The experiences
The time
Like the one
I spent at my Bua in pg Summer holidays of 2024
It was long, five weeks long, or I suppose to say one month long.
Last days at my Bua I felt constant stomach pain
Maybe it's because of food, or anxiety
Maybe it's because of staying longer at home without doing creative things like cooking my meal
Staying longer than a while has made my back and brain go to rest like some machine-catching virus
It's a mere stay which brings back memories of my stay in my hometown for two years and another two years
Once in lockdown of graduation
Twice for deciding my future through cuet
It feels like I am fading in the cold nights of 3:39 am
Memory fades, only residue stays.

22.7.2024

I had a dream this morning at 10:30 am
Filled with passion, anger and revolution,
I am with a guy named Zeeshan, his soft lips and
curly hair,
I drove him outside from the classroom of a Vedic
school mixed in Christian faith,
Announcing from the third floor, Mrs. J Or Z, "You
said I can't have a boyfriend. Let's see here he is. And
I am also not religious Phobic."
After Announcing, I pulled him from his collar, and
continued kissing his lips throughout the corridors of
the third floor that started in the classroom,
He couldn't stop either, he kept kissing, kissing, and
kissing, turning himself and me hard,
Until it's morning fall, an involuntary discharge.
I wake up.

While debating Language Politics In My Mind.

(Poem Written in Maithili)

कृष्ण आह त छी हर राधा के आस

नई बिसरब हमर एक झलक जब तक छी हम अई तट के दास

मछली से सनल इ घाट पुछल चंद्रमा से आहक पता हर बार

देखलउ सुनलउ हर ताना दिन रात

लेकिन कहलक एक जज्बात कि प्रेम नइ कोनो एहन घाट जे सुबह पसरल और शाम के समेटल साथ

There's A Coconut Tree Far…

There's a coconut tree far, 10 or 20 feet far from my house,
I have been watching it from my *baramda* since I was little,
It has been there for 24 years,
It has a life that I breathe,
But it gives that to me freely.
It is still there even though its Courtyard was turned into a local sweets factory *karkhana* some four or five years ago.
Houses changed from elvestered-roofs to terraces of soil, cement and brick,
Gali Ka Road changed from brickly to cemented,
Drainage changed from open to covered,
Gali Ka Road went up from being waterlogged for three to four days to being cleared few hours,
But it never changed it's the same old tree there.
My house transitioned from being two joint family to single,
From renters inhabiting our elvestered-rooftop house to that house being completely by itself, and becoming our storage room,
My Courtyard changed from an open bathroom to a closed bathroom with modern taps, showers 🪥 ,
From *chapakal* to moter, from *moter* to submersible following the water crisis,
From one tulsi and human temple— a simple white standing structure to a completely new red temple-like structure standing in a Courtyard to be prayed,

But it still is the same old tree, timeless, lifelong not
lifeless.
I wait every day watching it from my *baramda* or
open hall, now closed in steel or iron grill to avoid
monkeys, to know what it's like to be this free,
lifelong, breathing tree, home to coconut and many
birds.
What might freedom look like for a Young girl
peaking sun from the basement of the house,
What is the freedom for this Young boy watching the
moon in his Courtyard and dawn every day,
Perhaps nothing just a sublime beauty subverted away
from reality.

I watch the railway station from Harahi Lake
And think what freedom smells like far away across
country borders
Is it the same old cultural phobia, bullying, torture,
stereotypical judgements, homophobia, or is it a safe
place (one safe place from every Young guy and girl
Google history)?
Perhaps it's not that, perhaps, it's just a dream,
imaginative and fragile.
There's no freedom neither for a Young girl of the
20th century or a Young boy from the 21st century,
There's just a basement window and diary,
There's just an open Courtyard and pages of diary.
Imagine if she could have been given that freedom
what would life be for her,
Walking, singing, dancing on streets in rain or
Summer winds,
Or eating chocolates, ice cream, and food in
restaurants and local shops.
Or having met her only lover for eternity.

Or how openly reading books, schools, colleges,
university, graduate, masters, and doctoral.
Perhaps nothing just a sublime beauty subverted away
from reality.

MA Dissertation

I thought academia was all about Subjectivity and
subjective emotions,
There's no commonality, commoners, common
people, it's the academician eye searching for
evidence,
But it's all about objects and objectivity,
Considering the scene, all the academia based on the
basis of literary tradition already has answers,
On Monday, August 5, at 01:03,
I couldn't find any topic for the dissertation topic
because as I said the works have been written and told
already,
Is it death calling or the beginning of new trauma in
my living body?

Remembrance

On re-encountering Amrita Sher-Gill for my Masters
Dissertation:
People remember one who died very young
But that's the pre-colonial past and post-independence
lament of the 50s-60s
I live in the Age of AI
So I have to work a little harder
Stay a little longer
For my Remembrance.
- 12.07.2024 13:14

Evening Dream(ing) Poem while accepting the Nobel Peace Prize for a poem I wrote.

My Body is a women's adobe (abode).
It penetrate in viginal sofs.
In penatical muses.
In silence and excuses.

My Body is a women adobe,
It sees violence in sublime and social construction.
The skin falls on the ground
And The Muscles don't grow.
It reeks of a male and man of social construction.

My Body lacks priority.
It dilutes the thinness of the bone
And confuses it for non-binary.
I am male–a male of a binary
A variety among human male species.
I believe in the sexes.
Not in gender.
Gender is troublesome,
A chaos,
A suicide bomber in my country,
An another class difference penetrating through the
West.
Sex is an intersex,
A Hijra of the East,

A male, and a female desiring another male and
female.
Sexuality is five (Lesbian, Gay, Bisexual, Asexual
and Pansexual),
Not a million deaths.

Imagination Is Indian This Time

1. These days I often imagine myself standing on a
podium
Near Rashpati Bhavan area, closer to India gate
Braving new chapter in History---
A Bihari guy explaining the difference between
gender and sexuality
to millions of Gay souls this time not 10 thousand or
20.
How it is not exactly the same in the Indian context as
in the West,
How it's neither similar in the Indian context as in the
West,
Two cultures are rootedly different, socially and
Historically different.
Hence, gender as non-binary doesn't belong here.

What's non-binary?
Is it social factor or a psychological factor?
The nail polish, big and short hair, clothing (sari,
kurta, and suit-pant), bigger nails and shorter nails.
Or
The idea that one doesn't see themselves having
breasts (flattened and enlarged), penis and vagina on
their body.

Do they want change?
So is the division they are making on their body--- is
it because of social factors or psychological factors?

Is this social factor related to harm someone
perpetuated on their body? Is this what makes them
believe that their body is not of female and male, man
and woman binary?
Or
Is this psychological factor based on their feelings, a
emotions of liking to be in body they desired. The
concept of "Rooh making connection with atama"---
soul meeting body.

What is Transgenderism?
Is it the intersex body?
The one born with flattened breast and vagina. The
enlarged breast and penis. The variants of intersex
bodies. The (social and historical) mutilation they
suffered on their bodies as a teenager.
Or
Is the binary (male, man and female, woman) seeking
to convert themselves on basis of social or
psychological factor to idea of Trans body?

Who are Hijras?
Are they intersex babies thrown in the dustbin?
Are they girls?
Are they newly emerging trans identity?

2. Today at 22:15
I imagined myself interviewing only gay poet in
maithili
In his home.
In this home
My camera captures
The older aesthetic
Of his house, garden, courtyard (आँगन)

The poems he wrote In the backyard of his house, on terrace, on bed, in dinning room, in baramda*, and on his village trip.
The short-stories and novels, Novella celebrating liberating romance between two male bodies.

In the interview I ask him
To choose language to speak on camera
The option are English and Maithili
Or switching off and on between them.
English is for testimony of openness, rebel, freedom, the language that given voices over prejudices, the language the will give pride, an aesthetic appeal to all the background noises. The noises of homophobia, cultural shame, and साहित्यिक withdrawal of maithili community.
Maithili is the testimony for glory, a history, a Remembrance, a freedom of its language that speaks for everyone, the marginalized, the minor, the romantics, the reformer, the psychological mind, the body, the rain, the tree and how birds fly in the sky. A language going to write a new chapter in its hometown.

The poet chooses both
The reasons are Unknown
But I know why?
Because given the current status and cultural context of Homosexuality the camera appeals the Gaze of two. Drifting from either two is making people cringe.

3. I imagine two dead boys
Matting in the backyard of my house
Lacking visual representation.

I see no aesthetic in their death, love making, even in monochromatic Nokia videography.
This place is not "Calling me by your name", no Greek statue so closely in awe like some ancient Bard telling love songs.
This romanticism is so foreign to me. There was never one in India.
That's why when Call Be By Your Name ends on the television screen in my hometown room, it's almost evening, with sun shading yellowish-orange goodbye, there's a silence in my Courtyard.
I look at gods picture on the wall
I converse with them in my head
I points to picture and look into the chromatic videography camera of today.
At this moment there's an end to the aesthetic visual representation of myself in my house.

Home

What is home?
An eyelid lifting heavy night
Searching for sleep in the capital town.

A coconut tree
Standing far from my courtyard
Swamping away storms
Year after year.

What is home?
A middle class dreams
Fighting grammar in the classroom
of the school *Days*.

Rustling of the morning
Night
Afternoon
with fathers money collected from graves
while mother weeps you away
ironic it is her weeping
is your life frames.

What is home?
an independent cinema
starring konkona sen sharma
or commercial cinema that imtiaz ali has made.
A ticket counter
a theatre

movies that make friends.

A homie that you make
sucking cocks
or frotting of anxiety
in the light moron room or darker to avoid limelight.
A girl sucking boyfriend in the room
when her mother is gone
or CCTV that captures once in blood and thrones.
Is it same for everyone
Or is it Shame to be one.

What is home?
A fallen books from my hand
catching fire to look like exotic burns
in a closed rented apartment of 7k
because rates go high after that.

Or is it when i turn around
walk back to
search for american guy
asking him to marry me
And make me his continental state.

Home is what you make it
Is a classic lie
That one tells each other
Whenever they are shy.

Baby, you are not my cheerleader
Home is searching for you
go back to it
To loosen it up.

For those who are in capital towns

This is your new home.
a chapter
to remember in Afterlife.
घर एक सपना ही होता है।

What's funny in Woman?

On reading marathi gay novella Partner

What's funny in Woman
That people laugh and cry. [1]
What's funny in Woman
That people laugh and cry. [2]
Is the walk they carry
Or a lipstick they put on?
Is it the long breasts (pop culture 'boobs' and 'tits')
they put on?
Is it the uterus that manufactures babies every
generation
Or a vigina that gasps desires on their mythical
testosterone?
What's funny in Woman
Is the movement
The hand gestures
The eye rotation
Is it the curvy figure
The back that hits a million likes on Instagram post
Making them famous overnight?
What's funny in Woman
That man who drives like them
A man who desires another man
Men who have slight looks
The body
The born catish-walk
The soft skin
Are called Woman-like.

What's funny in Woman
That Men laugh at other Men
 Men who behave like woman
 Gets scared of being called out at public gatherings.
I believe I see these men
They are crying within
Carrying the burden of generational trauma
making woman their amusement
objects of desires
cry hours.
They need a healer,
Today when I finish writing this poem
I want you to close your eyes
And cry
let your shame wash away
in giving the woman of your dream a beauty.

मोन

1. बतहाँ छी रे|
अभगल कतक गेलऊँ तोहर भाग|
की छऊ तोहर राग|

2. मनोकामना
म+न+ओ+कामना
कामना
काम+ना

3. Cam Na
कम+मी+ना
कम+म+ई+न+आ

4. What's the difference?
Marriage-sex
Love-sex
Rape-sex

औरत
महिला
स्त्री

मर्द

पुरुष

पुरुख *(Maithili)*

Tirtiya Prakriti

त्रितीय प्रकृति

तृतीय प्रकृति

त+ऋ+त+इ

त+र्+अ

तीर

त+ई+र

प्रकृति

प्र+कृ+ति

प्र+क+र्+त+इ

Prakriti

प्राकृत

प्र+आ+कृ+त

प+र+अ+अ+क+ऋ+त

क+त्र+अ+त

कृत्य

क+त्र+अ+त्+य

Body who has been raped
is senseless.

Chapter 3: अंततः

Dear Reader,
If you have read the previous two chapters. Then read this in secrecy.
Yours truly,
असीम

1. "अहाँ केहन छी।," I asked the two passersby at
Darbhanga Junction.

"हां हम तँ ठीक छी। आँहा के बड़ दिन बाद देखलऊ हना।," They replied.

"I had been busy travelling to Delhi."

"अच्छा, अच्छा, इ बात छय।"

"Are you guys been together for a long time?"
"Longer enough than your English grammar
boyfriend."

"वो तो दो साल पहले ही मर गया।"

2. When I visit my Bua's house in Shalimar Bagh
I speak two languages.

और, केहन छला अहाँक हिमाचल के Trip?

 और, केसा था आपका हिमाचल का Trip?

Photo दिखाये ना.

3. की रे मौगा कि हाल छऊ?

किछु नई, हमर हाल की रहता।

हम तँ सब के देख रहल छी।

मर्द पत्ता, चूड़ा, और सब्जी बाइत रहल छैय।
औरत घर के अंदर खाना परोस रहल छैठीन।
हम मौगा घर के भीतर घुसल छी।

4. In my village
When I walk,
I see myself.
I see tall trees while my eyes watch
Birds flying from one tree
Making a cocoon-coco sound.
I see
The rustling of leaves
The sun setting in a yellowish-orange haze

The water in a lake splashed over my face.
Correction, I imagine water splashing over my face
That makes me laugh in shyness.
I imagine running across the sunflower field
While the camera videographs my monochromatic
moves.
I imagine running on the road, held by खेत on both

sides, sometimes leading me far and wide to a small
bridge hidden in the canopy of trees.
Sometimes small lakes make their way somewhere.
Sometimes to the Haunted stories of Rum-jaa or रमजा

बोर,

which I don't know
Because I never felt it.
It Summer end
I say goodbye to my village.

5. I saw a little guy cutting a tiny water bottle into
half making it a glass
He drinks water from it
From twenty-litter water cane
Is this a new story of my PG life I discovered at Ajay
Gas Service Shop at 11:17?

The Mid-20s

1. On visiting NSP Mela at the age of twenty-four
I see empty tiny white plates clatter on
the red carpet covered in dust.
left-over shops are selling street foods.

I experience a thrill of fear
On the big wheel
Someone said Ferris Wheel.
On the wooden boat ride
Some said the pirate ship was giving a pendulum
ride.
On the break dance
Where every breath breaks in between
And your head rushes through your body or is it the
opposite?
In Ferris Wheel your heart and head drop in lightness
from the above.
In the pendulum, your heart and head rise in the
lightness with every swing.
Then why this fear loops over
Is this sign of mid-20s
Or do you want to save yourself from Falling again in
the crowd watching?

2. On the eighteenth October
I walk in smoky weather
That's a light-hearted sun and white dust.
I walk when the shutter is down,

Street vendors selling Sabzi,
An open medical shop and atm,
And a police siren passes by.

I walk with my face down
Looking at my shoelaces
And white horizontal mercury light.
It's eight past twenty-three
When did that happen?
It was a few minutes ago
When I left my pg room.
It's Friday
And I find an empty metro,
Is it ironic or a surprise?
I want to ask myself "Why am I stressed?"
Is it the early hours of the day,
A presentation at the University.
Or Is it my father who phoned yesterday
To be alert for online money transfers to my sister's
university counter.

There's no rush on University Road today
It's calm and quiet.
Maybe it's vacation.

3. Is this stress and fear
Similar to a man loving another man
Or is it another symphony?

Domestic

If it is like this.
I can't help it has been the way it is.
If you have a time machine, you can change it. Well,
Try.

Why does a Woman wear makeup?
In a party, फंक्शन, and Wedding rituals.

Because they have beaten up their husband
And want to hide that beaten-up face and body,
With Bindi, lipstick, Mangalsutra, Har on the face
and Chiffon, Silk, and Cotton Saari on their body.
What are they hiding?
Is it their scars,
Is it hidden?
Is it their beauty,
Is it hidden?

How श्रंगार रसा
Became श्रंगार।

Or is it something they are covering up?
Is it their strength,
Is it covered up?
Is it their power to let go,
Is it covered up?

Why are they hiding and covering up?
To show the bravery of motherhood

To her Son,
To her children.
Or is that
She is too much dependent on Man
That she is projecting dependency on her Son.

How does their husband see her at parties, फंक्शन, and
Wedding rituals?
Like a Doll dressed up
Another traditional assumption, she is औरऽता।
Or they are just casual
हाँ, तिक ही तो है, जो है सो है।

Cycle

Husband beats his wife
Wife beats her Son
Son beats himself.

Husband beats his wife.
Wife hides herself.
Son returns from school and notices something fishy.
Son runs away from the house.

Husband beats his wife
smile
Son beats his wife.

Husband beats his wife.
Wife beats the shit out of herself.
daughter stops the father.
Son watches it.

Husband beats his wife.
Wife looks into her son's eyes.
Son is helpless.

Husband beats his wife.
Wife beats her Husband.
Daughter and Son run away inside the playroom.

Wife beats her husband.
Son watches from an upper-class balcony
and asks, "Is it right for a wife to beat her husband?"
It sparks gender debates.

Husband beats his wife.
Son watches tears coming out of her.
Son grows up to thirty.
Son has money.
Son stops his father.
Father stabs Son.
Son dies in his Courtyard.

Husband beats his wife.
Wife beats his husband.
Son Revolts.
Daughter watches it.
Husband And Wife are divorced.
They celebrate in America.

Chant Poem

पुम्प्रकृति
स्त्रीप्रकृति

त्रितीय प्रकृति

त्रिशूल

त्रिकोण

त्रिभूज

त्रिकाल

त्रिदेव

त्रि नेत्र

त्रिलिंग

त्रिलिंगूअल

फकरा: *"तीन तिगाड़ा काम बिगाड़ा"*

Langual
Lingual
Lang-uage

काल

क+अ+ल

कलि

क+ल+इ

काली

क+आ+ल+ई

कल्कि

क+ल्‌+इ+क

Binary opposition

दुविधा

द्विविजनल

ट्‌विलिंग

द्विलिंगूअल

Doubling
Dual Sexual

कलैशी

विनाशी

अविनाशी

फकरा:

नइ कोइ आश

नइ कोइ बास

नइ कोई घास

प्रकृति सँ भेल शब्द

शब्द भेल अपशब्द

अपशब्द भेल शब्द

शब्द भेल भाषा

भाषा भेल form

---

form se मिलल Hindavi
Hindavi मिलल फारषि सँ
बनल हिन्दी
हिन्दी देलक Meaning
Meaning सँ भेल कविता
कविता सँ भेल महाकवि।

अंग्रेज देलक अंग्रेजी
रेज के चयल गेल सीना।
अंग भेल त्रस्त
सिखलऊ English
घर पे बाजय छलऊ मैथिली
दुनु खेलक ठोकर
जुबान के भेल नौकर
नौकर छी हम गुलाम कँ
खोलब अब जबान।

[Insert Break]

Love Phobia

प्रेम-रोग
''शिव-सती''

अधूरी-मोहब्बत
''सलीम-अनारकली''

मनुस्मृति [4]
१ १.६८ ''पुरुष ने […] दूसरे पुरुष के साथ लैंगिक संबंध करना, इससे परंपरानुसार वह पुरुष जाती से बहिष्कृत किया जाता है|''

LovePhobia
''लड़का-लड़की''

''लड़की-लड़का''

''लड़का-लड़का''

''लड़की-लड़की''

Color Sexual

मत-भेदी

Color of Cultural Symbol
Color of Rituals
Color of skin
Color of Difference

भेद-भाव

अस्थायी

Migration
Invasion
Colonisation
Perversion
Death
Maddening
Silence
मोनी
प्रेम

जान-वर

Hunter and Huntress
Dwelling in a Jungle
One day saw sex
and have mangal.
They fuck out baby
And starts making gravy
Gravy becomes hot
Starts a talk
Talk becomes practice
Practice a Rituals
Rituals a norms
Norms so rigid
Catches the eye-wizards
Wizards do construction
(Helpless and Motivational)
Construction starts kingdom
Kingdom starts politics
Politics becomes body
Body play menstruation.
Menstruation ka Blood
भेल Survival

Survival का हुआ कचरा

ढुरलऊ अपन-अपन बछरा।

Rituals of Door

1.
Bell
Knock
Palm tap

        Closed
         Privacy
         Secrecy

Open
Watcher
Public

          Path
          Inside
          Outside

Woman watching Daily Soap
Is a cure for depression.
Man speak less
Is a quiet Sensation.

2.
There was a lake
In my maternal home
celebrating Chhath Puja
woman endowed with
Bangles, reddish lipstick,
saree yellow-green-red-pink
and young ladies in blue-green suits.
Young ladies got married

and Lake celebrates stills.
A boy at the Lake
is a watcher of the celebration.

Remembering

9:02, 11th November 2024

I witness a dream few minutes ago

In my maternal home

I am standing beside the bride-groom.

The happy Rasham रस्म

Bride laugh in her red lengha and choli

Groom smiles at her.

Something happens,

A camera turns a round,

Bride and Groom faces each other,

I and Bride runs away.

At few meters of running

We starts murmuring

Har din Ishq, Ishq, Ishq
Aree Ishq ke binap Azadi chahiye mujhe.

This dream was weird.

Was it telling me of Present,

Past-not lived, or Future?

        An old grandma said once something

        Which annoyed us furlong

        Why?

        Are we defiance of her touch

And quietness so rooted.

मैं सीता तेरे आँगन की।

Why say everything all at once?

Lets wait for time and tell.

        Jix, [19-11-2024 03:18]

        कृत्य

        काम

        मोक्ष

        Baby Eye

        |

        मर्द औरत का Eye

|

They are watching each other

|

जिज्ञासु बच्चन/छात्रपन/Adulthood/Parenthood

|

Manifesting in you

Had manifested in Parents

|

Is your कृत्य

|

Is your काम

|

Is your मोक्ष

|

Your मोक्ष Is your कार्य

|

कला का सम्मेलन/समर्थन/बाजार

|

सब कुछ एक ही है

|

वो है काम, मन से आया हुआ काम, मनोकामना

|

एक ही जीवन है, वो सबका अलग-थलग है

|

Don't compare yourself, your childhood
journey with your child's journey

|

Your Desire was to be an actor

|

It ends In 20th century

|

You became a Husband to a Wife

|

Her desire was to study

|

She became बोझ of child

|

बोझ से आहक मुक्ति केना मिलत, अपन-अपन
बचपन के कृत्य के समझु और आई के अस्तित्व
के जानु। आहक बचपन आहक बच्चा के बितल
शरीर दुनु अलग-थलग या।

|

My body is the meditation of my sexual energy, my body is meditation of desire, my body is the meditation of Kamana- मन की कामना।

|

It's manifestation is its individual journey. Its love is its individualistic-individualism.

हम अई से कहय छी कि अहा के दुखक कारण और कोई नई आहक कृत्य/कामना/मनोकमना या।

चलु एगो बात और कहावत में कहय छी-

वाणी के निर्लज्जता ककरोउ कतउ नई लोऊ जेत|
Your lingual violence can't walk you to you and yours child childhood home. Your affect is from both side.

Jix, [19-11-2024 03:59]

Who is Krishna Dvaipayana?

कृष्ण (Black Child) from Dvaipayana island from the child hood home travels to Kuru kingdom.

He watches कृत्य of everyone and wrote an epic literature.

महाभारतम्

To teach lessons to people.

B.R. Chopra made कृत्य टु Blame द्रोपती- वो 1990 काल के मर्द जात का आईना था।

Siddharth Anand Tiwari- ने अपने नाम का कृत्य निभाया।

Woman has individual journey. She is Savarni an individual महिला इन Vyas रचित वेदाह - शरीर का दहन/दान/spiritual healing.

Oral conversation to Written form.

प्राकृत भाषा से संस्कृत भाषा का आकार।

Indian English aam logo ki English Bhasa/Boli/Regional Dialect सँ अंग्रेजी भाषा का निर्माण।

Spoken English is Telling/Tale-ing English that which manifest itself in speech-act --- Body performs its poetry in its speech act. Master-Slave has given tension to village economy--- They started making sentences from the tense.

Then they started Bihari बच्चा/बाहर का बच्चा/ शहर का बच्चा टु गांव का बच्चपन।

आज दोनों का अस्तित्व clash Hota Hai. This is creating difference, violent mindsets and ab-use lingual-bodily behavior.

काला अकझर बैस बराबर।

काला रंग।

काली/कलि सबहक ध्यानाकर्षण करलु और जाननलु कतक छी हम।

In village journey my body, my eyes, my four senses travels from the dark midnight, seeing moons, trees, खेत in darkness to see लाईट of the city. My speech-acts its multilingual energy to thoughts that manifest on the keypad.

Jix, [19-11-2024 04:05]

Who is प्राकृति?

भाषा

Huntress womb Giving birth to baby.

Makes sounds of आकार।

• forms a meaning.

ऊ पेटक रचनात्मक रचनाकार- it tells a story.

Some childhood has advantages of living good life because they were born in the era after 2010s. Healthy nurtured baby. They have luckily great parenting.

Dear Childs father don't ab-use your historical advantages to ab-use other Childs childhood/Adulthood.

वेदाह मँ लिखल या pums prakriti/ stri prakriti/ tritiya prakriti

Napums Prakriti:

Kaliba: ka-li-ba

Iss prakriti ka रचनात्मक कोन?

जान-वर

Hunter-Hunteress

Pumps-स्त्री कृत्य

पु-लिंग/ स्त्री-लिंग

स्त्री पुरुष

मर्द औरत

महिला-पुरुष

त्रिलिंग

Perversion

Perverts

You'll are victim of your pervert culture?

Your Desire/कमना/मनोकमना comes from
the movies, films, cinema, songs, sangeet,
graphia you have watched in young days,
your touch is sensational/controversial
looping in your mind-sets.

ऐसा ही होता है क्यों?

Un-touched?
Un-touchable?
Un-?
Out-casting

शांत

शांत

शांत

Silence
Quiet

Does your town speak?
Yes, it speaks in stillness.

After finishing the poem (readers) sit in silence and
do चिन्तन।

Some Stills from CP, 20th November 2024 on the next page.

Returning Home.

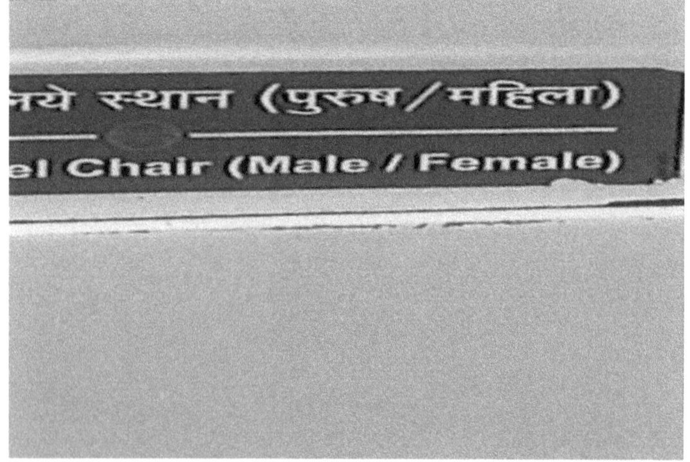

अहम् मुद्गलस श्रषि शान्तानम अस्ति?

After finishing the poem (readers) sit in silence and do चिन्तन।

Paint the book in your favourite color plates?

Iti-Hasa

(It thus happened?)

Say something new other then what
people are already saying?
One new thing?

If you haven't found anything new to
say?
i) This book doesn't belong to your
age?
ii) This book doesn't belong to your
कृत्य?
iii) This book doesn't belong to your
prakriti?

Is this desire yours?
Or Someone else? What was their
desire as a child?

Chapter 4: *Re-Verse*

Dear असीम,

Some notes for your looping 30ish self

I am in the loop--- of life stories told by my parents.

I lost 1,217 rupees while ordering a book.

I have imagined a lot about hooks.

So much so that it led me to consciously dying imagery.

I belong to a land of history. *KamaSutra* is one of them. The desires loop in its atmosphere.

Several books, Quizzes, and Competition. None to be taken care of.

I possibly couldn't imagine the severity. Neither can work in variety.

So, how should I recover money; I have emailed them.

I had a fight with Queer Ink on chats—they missed calls of a male body out-casting from its queer culture.

Publishing legality and ventures. Is it all the same as my timeline? Or is it another new story of a man who loves a man?

There are so many Telling/Tale-ing poems happening in India.

Why are they telling? Whom are they telling?

A colonial-mind sets or Pervert culture.

Or their homely parents to see what it is?

Your, "जो है सब यही है" has found an answer.

On the footpath of the capital.

This American Gen Z membership is expiring.
Welcome to Gen-Milliz membership.
The transformational and transgenerational locality.
What are you gaping in the east-west divide?
What are you trying to fixate on?

www.ingramcontent.com/pod-product-compliance
Lightning Source LLC
Chambersburg PA
CBHW040124150726
48005CB00015B/2363